GOD
Believes in

Jewelry

GOD
Believes in

R. E. Francis
with George E. Vandeman

Pacific Press Publishing Association
Boise, Idaho
Oshawa, Ontario, Canada

Designed by Tim Larson
Cover photo by Joan Walter

Library of Congress Cataloging in Publication Data

Francis, R. E. (Robert E.), 1917-
  God believes in jewelry.

  1. Jewelry—Religious aspects—Seventh-Day Advent-
ists. 2. Seventh-Day Adventists—Doctrines. I.
Vandeman, George E. II. Title.
BX6154.F665   1984   241'.674   84-25462

ISBN 0-8163-0590-0

  92 93 94 • 8 7 6 5

But the father said to his servants, Bring forth the best robe, and put it on him; and put a ring on his hand, and shoes on his feet. Luke 15:22.

God Believes in Jewelry

I was seventeen and not a Christian. By chance—no, I don't believe it was by chance—I wandered onto the campgrounds of the Pennsylvania Conference of Seventh-day Adventists during their camp-meeting session. I gazed at the people at this religious gathering with mixed emotions. I knew very little about the Bible and practically nothing about Seventh-day Adventists. I had rings on my fingers, cigarettes in my pocket, and a great curiosity about these strange, plain-looking people.

As I stood there, no doubt with a bewildered look on my face, a young fellow not quite out of his teen years came up to me and introduced himself.

"I'm George Vandeman," he said.

After telling him my name, I asked about these people who seemed so different. Plain. No jewelry. Very little, if any, make-up! Perhaps it was this conversational point of interest that caused him to pursue this subject with me.

We became fast friends. The young man who was influential in bringing me to Christ and the Seventh-day Adventist Church was the now well-known TV evangelist, George Vandeman. Very soon he began giving me Bible studies, and one of the most interesting studies I ever received was on the subject of jewelry.

"I can't believe," I said, "that God doesn't want people

to look their very best." I looked down at the rings on my fingers. "Why doesn't God want Seventh-day Adventists to wear jewelry? They look so plain!"

George smiled understandingly. "God," he said, "is a great jeweler. The Bible tells us that the New Jerusalem has streets of gold and gates of pearl. What a city!"

My new friend certainly had a knowledge of Scripture. I listened intently as he went on. He took me to heaven via the Scriptures. He introduced me to Lucifer, a happy, holy, harmless angel, who was covered with jewels. I looked at George in surprise as he read, for I had always thought of heaven as being a place where everyone wore a halo and a white robe—but no jewelry. No jewelry for sure!

But there it was in the Bible. "Thou [Lucifer] sealest up the sum, full of wisdom, and perfect in beauty. Thou hast been in Eden the garden of God; every precious stone was thy covering, the sardius, topaz, and the diamond, the beryl, the onyx, and the jasper, the sapphire, the emerald, and the carbuncle, and gold." Ezekiel 28:12, 13.

Next he brought me down to earth and read to me about Aaron, the high priest. The only place in Scripture where God specifically outlined what a person was to wear is in the high priest's dress.

I was pointed to his jewels as recorded in Exodus 28. There was a breastplate of gold on which twelve large precious stones were set in sockets of gold. Added to these were two large onyx gems, one on each shoulder. And these two gemstones were encircled by six each of the twelve which occupied the breastplate. A golden mitre or crown rested upon his head.

Beautiful! Dignified! The colors of gold, blue, red, and white exquisitely arranged upon his person! He stood out distinctively. God deliberately planned it to be this way. George made it clear that God was the Designer!

"If God is a jeweler, if God's Holy City is so liberally endowed with jewels, if God's servants, Lucifer in heaven and Aaron on earth, were so resplendently bejeweled—at God's own direction—why is jewelry so conspicuous by its absence among these Seventh-day Adventists?" I queried.

My young instructor was quick to suggest that the jewels of Lucifer and Aaron were designed to reflect certain characteristics of God. Lucifer was in character to some degree what his jewels represented God to be. Does gold represent righteousness?[1] Lucifer had both. Does the blue of the sapphire represent loyalty, true-blue loyalty?[2] Lucifer had both. Hence Lucifer could wear these jewels meaningfully. He was in good taste in an unfallen society, living as he did in the presence of God, the Great Jeweler!

"But Lucifer sinned,"[3] said George. "Lucifer walked out of the glory.[4] His hallelujahs ceased. The situation changed. 'Ichabod!' (the glory is departed) was now heard. The glory-to-God intent of the jewels had vanished, tints and tones. And, if he were to wear them now—in his sin—it would be hypocrisy. He would be falsely advertising those spiritual qualities *not* represented by his jewels. The best they could now do for him would be to satisfy a fleeting attempt at self-glorification."

George continued, "When God is depicted in the Bible as putting jewelry on His people, it is symbolic of a holy character or the changed character He develops in us. When we put jewelry on ourselves, it is an indication that we are trying to do for ourselves that which only God can do."

I cast a glance at the rings on my fingers. A feeling of uneasiness arose within me. The reality of my motives began to surface. A sense of spiritual perception put me on a collision course with my real self. I knew I had not consulted God or His glory in the wearing of the rings on my fingers.

"Couldn't jewelry be worn symbolically?" Now I was on the defensive. "There's the Masonic ring with its G for God, the ring of high-school achievement, the ring of athletic championship, the ring of marital memorial, etc."

"Yes, you could," Vandeman replied. "But then it would be a matter of priorities, wouldn't it?" he cautioned.

"I'm not sure I understand what you mean?"

"Human custom or God's will—which should have the preference?"

"But," I reflected upon the many good Christians who wear jewels, "it seems to me I read somewhere where a ring was put on the prodigal son's finger." My jewels were in jeopardy now. It became clear I would not let them go without a struggle.

Then in measured, even tones George Vandeman proposed, "Having shown that Lucifer and Aaron wore jewels, would you like to look at some reasons why Seventh-day Adventists do not apply those reasons to themselves? Why Seventh-day Adventists minimize the external use of jewelry?"

Yes, I thought, that would be interesting. Most other professed Christians wear jewelry. Why not Seventh-day Adventists?

George proposed five reasons.

1. The Jesus' Example Reason

George opened his Bible and read about Christ's "leaving us an example, that [we] should follow his steps."[5]

"You mean an example to us for *not* wearing jewelry?" I inquired, somewhat puzzled, that he could read jewelry into this Scripture.

10

"Very much so," was his reply. "Think of Jesus as God, Almighty God, with infinite glory and power. Then think of a time when this same Jesus lays aside this glory, walks off the streets of gold, away from the gates of pearl—to become a creature of the dust, a man, the God-man. In a manner of speaking, one could say, as He walked out of this glory, He *took off* 'His jewels.' He certainly left behind a literal paradise full of them, wouldn't you say?"

I nodded. That part was too obvious.

He then turned to Philippians 2:5-8 and said to me, "Here, Bob, you read this." And he added, "It speaks to the point you raised."

I read, "Let this mind be in you, that was in Christ Jesus."

He interjected, "And, of course, the mind of Jesus as our example lays aside personal glory, doesn't it? But, read on, Bob, there's more."

I continued, "Who being . . . God . . . made himself of no reputation, and took upon him the form of a servant, . . . and became obedient unto death."

"That's example, Bob. That's real example involving many areas of conduct." After a short pause he suggested, "It could even suggest the form of a servant—without rings!"

Then he made his point. "You asked whether Jesus was an example to us concerning jewels. Well, if as a follower of Jesus, 'I am crucified *with* Christ,'[6] not being 'conformed to this world,'[7] but rather walking 'as he walked,'[8] crying out, 'Nothing in [or on] my hands I bring, simply to Thy cross I cling,' the question arises, Does earthly jewelry fit into the mind of Jesus working in me and you?"

This came to me as a startling discovery. I was not prepared to think this way—the King of jewels without jewels! I thought for what seemed a long time about this.

11

George paused, letting this spiritual truth penetrate. With deliberate, slow emphasis he said softly, and his words pulled on me, "Lest you think Jesus' example has little to do with our earthly ornamentation, consider this: at the cross evil men cast lots for Jesus' quality garment (probably given to Him), yet no lots were cast for His jewels. Apparently *there were none*! In the light of these scriptures, when it comes time for you and me to die, what will be found among our earthly goods? If we have had the mind of Jesus, what will be left to divide of our possessions?"

I began to see something of the meaning of inward jewelry. And I heard George saying, "When it comes to jewels, jewelry, ornamentation, there is no greater example to follow in this world of sin than that of Christ's."[9]

Now, years later, I reflect upon the point George made of Jesus' example. And a text comes into my mind, "Not every one that saith unto me, Lord, Lord, shall enter into the kingdom of heaven; but he that doeth the will of my Father." Matthew 7:21.

Although I was not a Seventh-day Adventist back then, George had stimulated my thinking. At that time I was not yet ready to decide on these things. So I suggested, evasively, "Didn't you say you had some other reasons?"

"Yes," he responded tactfully, "there is a second reason for the Seventh-day Adventist attitude toward jewelry. It is the I-Am-Responsible-for-My-Influence Reason."

2. The I-Am-Responsible-for-My-Influence Reason

I was directed to 1 Corinthians 8. The reason involved in this chapter was the most provocative of all the reasons George proposed. Because, in effect, it said, I won't do what I feel I could do. That is to say, I can eat this or wear that, but I won't. Why not? Because it may confuse the

12

faith of another person. Therefore, I will exercise the mind of Christ within me to sacrifice that which may be perfectly all right if it causes others to stumble.

George briefly explained this chapter—food offered to idols; young Christians disturbed; idolatrous food eaten; confusion in the church. He pointed out that Paul felt he could eat this food inasmuch as the food itself had not been altered by any such heathen ceremony. Newly converted pagans did not see this as clearly as Paul did. It was Paul's enlightened intelligence versus their superstitious ignorance. They were steeped in heathen traditions. They were mere babes in the faith. Then, when other Christians ate of this idol food, these babes in the faith became confused. Paul saw that these weak brethren needed protection and nurturing more than to have their sensibilities shocked.

So Paul presented to the Corinthian church the influence-responsibility principle of 1 Corinthians 8. The essence of it is, "if what I eat causes my brother to fall into sin, I will never eat meat again [food offered to idols], so that I will not cause him to fall."[10]

In other words, Paul could, but wouldn't. (Notice his use of the word *again* in this text.) He esteemed the welfare of his unenlightened brother a greater necessity than his own privilege of eating this food. "This," said George, "is assuming responsibility for one's influence! It is saying, I will endure inconvenience for myself before I will become a stumbling block to my brother."

He pointed out to me that a broadened paraphrase of this principle could read, "I will no longer wear rings while the world lasts, lest I confuse my brother or sister in matters concerned with jewelry."

This influence-responsibility principle more than any of the other reasons George mentioned, if applied, could go a long way toward resolving many of the problems facing

Christians today. It brings the Christian into the mainstream of Christ's own lifestyle. It ministers as a servant to others, rather than one ministering to himself. It speaks to the text, "I am crucified *with* Christ." It is a Christ-in-you thing lived out. It is doing righteousness by God's grace without a tinge of legalism involved. It is Moses saying to God, "Blot my name out of Thy book, if you blot out these Israelites."[11] In short, it takes the rings off—for the sake of others.

My young teacher now read from a small book by Ellen G. White. "The spirit of Christ's self-sacrificing love is the spirit that pervades heaven and is the very essence of its bliss. This is the spirit that Christ's followers will possess."—*Steps to Christ*, p. 77.

"Look at its built-in spiritual principles." George added, "With Jesus it says, 'When asked for your coat, give your cloak also. When asked to go one mile, go two.'[12] It is esteeming others better than yourselves. It is putting God first, others second, yourself third. This is practical love, lovingly practiced.

"Here is the basic reason why Jesus walked off the streets of gold. This is why there is no record of His wearing any jewelry while here on earth. The vast majority of humanity can't wear it because they can't afford it, so He didn't. Thus He identified with us. He met us on our own jewel level, as it were—without jewels—so that one day we can wear heaven's crown jewels. He wore thorns here that we might wear gold there!" This is how George explained the influence-responsibility principle.

"But George," I cried out, "how far does one go in inconveniencing himself for another's welfare? After all, there are altogether too many people with hangups. Too many people are confused about too many things. How can you please them all?"

"True," he agreed. "But, remember this, Bob, God

promises to give you His Holy Spirit to guide you in such situations. Jesus prayed to His Father who sent the Holy Spirit to 'guide . . . [Him] into all truth.'[13] This promise is available to you and me."

I began to see that with gospel privilege comes gospel responsibility. I saw they could not be separated, for I am my brother's keeper. To "take up my cross and follow Christ,"[14] seems to be a restatement of the 1 Corinthians 8:13 influence-responsibility principle.

I began to see my rings in relation to others in the light of Christ's cross in relation to me. This principle convicted me deeply. I was beginning to see that with the love of Jesus in my heart, it was possible for me to make nonlegalistic sacrifices for others I never dreamed possible. A broader, deeper view of the Christian life opened before me. I shall be eternally grateful to young George Vandeman for this eye-opener. Now I can see more clearly how the responsibility aspect of the gospel can indeed be helpful in preserving the faith of the babes in the faith. I can also see how it can be instrumental in effecting unity within the church. But it takes the Spirit of Jesus within the heart. Without the Spirit of God, we most certainly will rationalize or philosophize away the solid biblical reasons for Jesus' attitude regarding jewelry. George moved on to his third reason.

3. The Consecration Reason

"The Bible links jewelry to one's sense of consecration or lack of it. Did you know that, Bob?" he asked.

"No," I replied. I wore it because *I* liked it. It appealed *to me*. I was caught up in the popular custom of wearing it. I did not have God in mind in the wearing of it.

George pointed out that when the Holy Spirit convicts a person of sin, there arises in the honest heart a desire to

15

reconsecrate himself to God, to get things straightened out. The Bible, he stated, gives many instances where jewelry is associated with this consecration effort.

He told me the story of Dinah's defilement and of Jacob's sons murdering the Shechemites. So bad was the situation that Jacob cried out, "Ye cause me to stink"[15] in the community. Jacob saw the necessity for an immediate consecration-revival meeting. Here's what happened: "Then Jacob said unto his household, and to all who were with him, Put away the strange gods that are among you, and be clean. . . . And they gave unto Jacob all the strange gods which were in their hands, and all their earrings which were in their ears; and Jacob hid them under the oak which was by Shechem." Genesis 35:2-4.

George said that some feel that strange gods and the jewelry are not the same things. However, Jacob linked them together in the consecration service, because the Bible says he hid them *both,* the gods and the jewels, under that Shechem oak tree. Obviously he planned for them to stay there! George called my attention to this fact. Certainly digging them up later would betray the sincerity of their consecration! His logic was compelling.

Then he took me to Mount Sinai with its golden-calf worship.[16] God and Moses were displeased. God directed Moses to conduct a revival. In the ensuing consecration meeting, the Israelites were told to "put *off* thy ornaments. . . . And the children of Israel *stripped themselves of their ornaments.*"[17]

Now, years later, I think in retrospect of Seventh-day Adventists. I ask myself, Do we need such a consecration? What kind of aroma are we creating? Is there infidelity in our marital and social relationships? If so, what false gods and what jewelry do we need to bury under our oak tree? Is it possible that there is shadiness in some of our financial dealings? Is there indulgence in sex and

16

drugs in our camp? Are there strange gods and jewelry we should bury under that oak tree? Talk about jewelry! There are many oak trees beckoning for our consecration today!

Moses didn't have a literal oak tree in the desert at Sinai. So what did he do? At God's direction, he ground up the golden calf, mixed it with water, and made the Israelites drink it. In that consecration meeting, golden calf, jewelry, and strange gods were decisively stripped away. Talk about jewelry! Sinai awaits us today! And especially so as we look at jewelless Calvary!

4. The Comparison Reason

George warmed to his next topic, the Comparison Reason. "If the Lord were to come today," he said, "there would be only two classes of people to meet Him." He listed them: the ready and the unready, the just and the unjust, the gold and the dross, the wheat and the tares. He reduced the two classes to the two groups of Zion and Babylon.

I was mystified. "What do you mean, 'Zion and Babylon?' "

"Zion," replied George, "is a biblical expression for God's people." He quoted the scripture, "Zion, Thou art my people."[18] He further showed God's people were likened unto "a comely and delicate woman."[19]

"Of course," he explained "Zion itself comes in two packages also." He read to me of the one group in Zion who were "washed,"[20] "comely,"[21] "modest," not ornamented "with gold, or pearls,"[22] but rather possessing "the ornament of a meek and quiet spirit."[23]

I caught the picture of purified gold, wheat ready to harvest, the saints of God accepted of Him and bearing fruit to His glory.

17

Then he read to me of the other group in Zion. They, by contrast, were unwashed,[24] "haughty," and with "wanton eyes,"[25] wearing leg ornaments, along with headbands, earrings, and rings.[26] There was no mistaking this group. Here was the dross, the tares, the mixed multitude within Zion. Of course these represented the Babylonian side of Zion. Behold the wheat and tares growing together within the church until the harvest!

He showed me the contrast between earth's last-day Zion, the woman of Revelation 12, and modern Babylon's harlot woman of Revelation 17. George said, "The woman of Revelation 12 is robed in an all-white gown." She has no literal jewelry on her person except a symbolic crown of twelve stars, emblematic of her tie-in with the twelve apostles and their victorious faith. She herself is a living jewel. She is God's Zion in our day.

Then there is the modern-day harlot of Revelation 17. She stands in sharp contrast to true Zion. There the harlot woman stands, clad in scarlet and purple, decked with gold and precious stones. Significantly, in her hand is a wine glass full of abominations!

"See the contrast!" George exclaimed. "Two different types of characters! Two different types of dress! Two different types of jewelry! And for two different purposes! One reflects Jesus in her heart; the other scintillates on the outside!"

I wasn't aware that was in the Bible. I was surprised. I pictured myself in both camps. I had mixed emotions about what I was learning. It was all so new. A conflict was beginning to churn within me. My heart told me George was right. My carnal self felt defensive, disturbed, threatened.

As I was musing within myself, my young teacher said to me, "Incidentally, Bob, did you know that Aaron, God's high priest, on the day of atonement (tenth day of

18

the seventh month of each year), *took off* all of his many jewels, including his crown of gold? When he appeared before God, as it were, in the most holy place, he did so in the white linen robe of the common priest. His only jewels, you might say, were spiritual ones—those developed by Christ within his heart's temple. And even these were covered by this common white robe, symbolic of Christ's righteousness.

"This depiction of Aaron before God, as representative of God's Zion, God's people, tells the story of Adventist attitudes toward jewelry. This, by faith, is how we should look today. Not in Aaron's high-priestly garb, not even literally in Aaron's common-priestly garb, but most certainly in the robe of Christ's righteousness and with 'the ornament of a meek and quiet spirit' within. This is the acceptable jewelry for God's saints today."

He paused for emphasis. "Spiritual jewelry, unseen but by God, this is what God wants for us today."

I was in a listening mood. The place and purpose of spiritual things began to crystallize in my mind. Like the woman at the well, I found myself wanting more.

Perceiving my deepening interest, George continued, "We, as Seventh-day Adventists, believe we are living in the day of atonement in the heavenly sanctuary for our day. Aaron's earthly sanctuary pointed to our day. We believe, by God's grace, we should now be making a heart preparation for our Lord's return. We feel we should be seeking after the inner adornment that Peter and Paul talked about: "Whose adorning let it not be that outward adorning of plaiting the hair, and of wearing of gold, or of putting on of apparel; but let it be the hidden man of the heart, in that which is not corruptible, even the ornament of a meek and quiet spirit, which is in the sight of God of great price." 1 Peter 3:3, 4. "In like manner also, that women adorn themselves in modest apparel, with shamefacedness and sobriety; not with broided hair, or gold, or pearls, or costly array." 1 Timothy 2:9.

"You see, Bob," he explained, "we are to come out from Babylon and be separate,[27] not as gazingstocks and oddballs, no. These texts are not inconsistent. There is a beautiful logic in them. They tell us to *put on modest apparel*, while *taking off* the outward adornment of gold or pearls, even of unduly costly array. They tell us to *put on* the spiritual adornment in the heart.

"The inherent idea of these Scriptures is to give to the saints of God the Christ-within look. God is to be glorified, not us. There is to be a clear distinction between God's Zion and the world's modern Babylonians. We should be as distinctively different from modern Babylonians as were Daniel and his three Hebrew companions when compared to their ancient Babylonian associates. They are to be distinct from tares as is the wheat, the sheep from the goats, gold from dross. Jesus will not come again until His character is perfectly reproduced in His people. When this happens all will know who wears God's real jewelry."

5. The Translation Reason

There is a group of people who will see the Lord coming in glory and will be translated to heaven without seeing death. Though once unregenerated sinners,[28] they now, like Elijah, by the grace of God, have been transformed, never to die. They stand unafraid, unashamed amidst the devouring elements when the glory of the Lord flashes forth at His second coming. They go through the "time of trouble, such as never was."[29] They stand unharmed amidst the glory light that destroys the wicked.[30] They say, "Lo, this is our God . . . and he will save us."[31] But the wicked call for the rocks and moun-

20

tains to hide them from His face. There is a marked contrast.

George briefly explained to me this awesome time. Then he continued, "Let us assume for argument's sake that these final saints are wearing rings and other jewelry and that they see no 'wrong' in these earthly attachments. And now with these ornaments all aglow, Jesus comes! What then?"

I nodded assent. He continued,

"Bob, I want to read a scripture; then I want to ask you some questions."

He turned to Isaiah 65:17 and read, "I [God] create new heavens and a new earth: and the former shall not be remembered, nor come into mind."

Of course he made it clear that the saints will know each other on that other shore. He pointed out that there "shall I know even as also I am known."[32] But the egotistical, evil things of earth will have been erased.

Probably George had this new earth scene in mind as he read the following description from Ellen G. White: "Here [in paradise restored] we saw the tree of life and the throne of God. . . . We all went under the tree and sat down to look at the glory of the place, when brethren Fitch and Stockman, who had preached the gospel of the kingdom, and whom God had laid in the grave to save them, came up to us and asked us what we had passed through while they were sleeping (in the grave). We tried to call up our greatest trials, but they look so small compared with the far more exceeding and eternal weight of glory that surrounded us that we could not speak them out, and we all cried out, 'Alleluia, heaven is cheap enough!' and we touched our glorious harps and made heaven's arches ring."—*Early Writings*, p. 17.

George built up to his next point. "Imagine," he said, "every trace of sin is swept away. All things earthly such as we have known them here are gone. Only one reminder remains, the marks of Jesus' crucifixion."

Having established this picture of earth's last generation of saints who are now in paradise restored, he posed these questions in the light of Isaiah 65:17:

"1. If these last Elijah-type saints are wearing earthly rings, etc., as Jesus comes the second time, will they wear them in paradise restored?

"2. If these jewels are worn in paradise restored, what purpose will they serve there?

"3. If they are *not* worn there, *when* will they be removed? Will they be taken off *in transit* to the holy city by the saints themselves? Or will their attending angel tactfully suggest that the saints take them off, inasmuch as they are no longer relevant in that better and far different land?

"4. If they are taken off before entry into paradise restored, what is the reason for so doing? And, why cannot that reason be applied *now*, if, indeed, now we are preparing for citizenship in that better land and have the mind of Jesus here?"

I conceded the point. I had nothing to say. At that time, being young and a participant in the good, old American, red-blooded game of football, I saw the ridiculousness of wearing in heaven a ring that memorialized a stalwart gallop for a touchdown for the good old Maroon and White of the Tiffin Jr. O. U. A. M. High School!

I could see that the old clichés, "I don't see anything wrong with it," "We live in a new age," "Everybody's doing it," were totally inadequate for one who was heaven and homeland bound.

I paused. "George," I managed to say, "you are really telling me, 'Better to take them off now than later,' aren't you?"

We smiled at my candor and his subtle tact. Today,

years later, I ponder that scene. Why should I put on *after* my baptism that which I took off before I was baptized! As one who looks to Jesus as his Example and desires to be translated, I am convinced that He is the only jewel I need.

These biblical concepts pointed up the fact that I am responsible for my influence. Seeing these reasons as biblically and spiritually established, I have long since agreed with my young teacher's reasoning. Indeed, having taught academy and college students for nearly forty years, I am more convinced than ever that these are truths for us as a people, even in our day. The gospel of Jesus should make a marked difference between His remant people and worldings, without making the former appear as oddballs.

George closed his Bible, dropping his arms to his side. He had given his reasons as a Seventh-day Adventist for his faith in God, the Great Jeweler.

Neither of us spoke. In the brief silence I must have been nervously twisting the rings on my fingers. There we sat, each with his own thoughts.

Finally George spoke. "May I see your rings, Bob?"

I took them off.

He held them up. "Gold," he muttered, "and a topaz."

"Yes," I murmured, "sort of sentimental, I guess." I was unsure of myself.

"I understand," he replied softly. "And the Pearl of Great Price! What about Him? Here is *real* sentiment, Bob, with *real* meaning. Don't you agree?" He slightly accented the word *real*.

He handed my rings back to me. Then looking me squarely in the eye, and with some feeling said, "You seem to have some concern about the real meaning of jewelry, don't you?"

Again his words tugged on me.

"Of course, the decision is yours," was his appeal. I knew he was right. I was intellectually convinced in spite of myself. And in my heart I saw a bit of the preciousness of the spiritual truth involved. The Holy Spirit was surely moving upon my heart. I never expected this when I started the discussion. I had a new insight into the mentality of Seventh-day Adventists.

I put the rings into my pocket. George smiled. So did I. In time I was given more studies by Elder Dallas Youngs on other subjects even more important than jewelry. These other foundational subjects should have come first. But George saw my need. He met me on the ground of my current interest. He was helpful in creating in me, by God's grace, an appreciation of a whole new vista of life's broader, deeper values.

Later I surrendered to Christ, the Great Jeweler. He is the one who engineers human jewelry out of their miry clay. Having surrendered to Him, I never felt it was necessary to put on the rings which I took off when George asked, "May I see your rings, Bob?"

Since becoming an Adventist I have learned that when Jesus comes the second time in great glory, He will be coming for His jewels.[33]

God's idea of jewelry for His church in this sinful world is clear. He prefers that she adorn herself with Himself in her heart's temple. And this is all the jewelry she needs! Indeed, the absence of it upon the person of the modern Seventh-day Adventist will provide a wonderful opportunity to give the "Vandeman reasons" for *not* wearing it. Rather than being defensive and conforming to the situation, why not be evangelistic?

It is true, God is a Great Jeweler. His priority now seems to be to burnish and polish His human jewelry; then later in paradise restored, make available to them the treasures of heaven. See Him at work as He transforms

His creatures of dust. See those steeped in wordliness re-made into human gold many times purified from sin.[34] See His smile as He envisions them one day walking the streets of gold, in and out of the gates of pearl. They wear a crown of gold that will not fade away.

What About Those Crowns of Gold in Heaven!

The following paragraphs are taken from *The Great Controversary*, pages 647, 648. Emphasis supplied.

"As the ransomed ones are welcomed to the City of God, there rings out upon the air an exultant cry of adoration. The two Adams are about to meet. The Son of God is standing with outstretched arms to receive the father of our race—the being whom He created, who sinned against his Maker, and for whose sin the marks of the crucifixion are borne upon the Saviour's form. As Adam discerns the prints of the cruel nails, he does not fall upon the bosom of his Lord, but in humiliation casts himself at His feet, crying: 'Worthy, worthy is the Lamb that was slain!' Tenderly the Saviour lifts him up and bids him look once more upon the Eden home from which he has so long been exiled.

"The Saviour leads him to the tree of life and plucks the glorious fruit and bids him eat. He looks about him and beholds a multitude of his family redeemed, standing in the Paradise of God. *Then he casts his glittering crown at the feet of Jesus*, and falling upon His breast, embraces the Redeemer. He touches the golden harp, and the vaults of heaven echo the triumphant song: 'Worthy, worthy, worthy is the Lamb that was slain, and lives again!' *The family of Adam take up the strain and cast their crowns at the Saviour's feet* as they bow before Him in adoration."

The saints will wear these crowns of gold as memorials of their victory over sin *through Christ*! But let us never forget that the crown as a symbol, even though it be literal gold, falls far short of what it symbolizes! In Christ's presence the golden crown fades into nothingness for *He* is our Righteousness! *He* is our salvation! *He* is our glory! *He* is the Pearl of Great Price! *He* is the Great Jeweler who made your crown and gave it to you as a gift— forever!

Yes, the symbol is never equal to what it symbolizes in the sense that we would never trade the crown for Jesus Himself. The symbol of faith can never be as valuable as the faith it symbolizes. We will always cast our crowns at Jesus' feet! Even in heaven!

"Seek ye first the kingdom of heaven" here on earth; that is, seek ye first to adorn the heart's temple with Christ within it and all these things (Paul's "henceforth" a crown) will be added to you in that earth made new!

God is indeed a Great Jeweler. He really believes in jewelry!—at the right time, in the right place, for the right purpose!

Excuses for Wearing Jewelry Today

The following are some excuses that some people make for wearing jewelry. They are followed by scriptural answers:

"Others are doing it."
(But read John 21:22, 23; Proverbs 21:2; Exodus 23:2; and 1 Kings 19:10, 18.)

"It's the custom now."
(But read Matthew 15:1-9; Romans 12:2; 1 John 2:15, 16; and 1 Samuel 8:5-9.)

"We live in a new enlightened age."

(But read Isaiah 60:2; Matthew 24:11, 12, 24; Amos 5:20; Joel 2:1, 2; and 2 Timothy 3:1-9.)

"A ring was put on the prodigal son's finger."
(But read, asking, What kind of ring? For what purpose? If God puts jewelry on us, it is as an evidence that He has changed our characters and our status with respect to Himself; but if we put it on ourselves, it is an evidence that we are trying to do that which only God can do. SDA BC, vol. 5, p. 821; and Esther 8:2.)

"God put jewelry on Lucifer."
(But read where God takes it off: Ezekiel 28:16-19.)

"God put jewelry on Aaron."
(But read where Aaron takes it off: Exodus 32 and 33.)

"I don't see anything wrong with it."
(But read 1 Corinthians 8:9-13; Proverbs 14:12; and Luke 22:42.)

"There is no moral significance in a jewel."
(But when associated with Christians it has influence, [see 1 Corinthians 8:9-13] and responsibility [see Genesis 4:9]. *Therefore*, it does have moral significance!)

Other Excuses

There are some things God permits that He doesn't want. He permits this in the case of those who are honestly ignorant of His will. (See Acts 17:30) However, with those who know His will but use His mercy as an excuse for disregarding what they know to be His will, it is a different matter. Anyone who knowingly goes contrary to His will is taking a dangerous course.

For example, God permitted Israel to have a king. Not only did He not want Israel to have a king, but He warned them against such. God wanted undisputed first place for Himself—as directly connected with His people as possible in their sinful condition. This "new" arrangement was God's best plan for sinner-man. And it called forth from them best-plan faith!

The installation of King Saul was, by comparison, a second-best plan. There was danger here. The exercise of their faith would tend to gravitate to this second-best level. The unique, peculiar path God had chosen for His people would become obscured, clouded.

And it did! Israel, in time, moved toward the everchanging, shifting sands of the moods and fads of the world. They became more and more like the nations round about, so much so that ultimately they cried out, "We have no king but Caesar!" Second-best became nothingness!

Then there is the example of divorce. God, we are told, allowed it "because of the hardness of your hearts." That's second best. Because "from the beginning it was not so."[35]

What about the wedding ring? Under what "plan" would it come? It has no biblical basis in fact, either by precept or by example. It is admittedly pagan in origin. It derives its credibility solely from human culture and practice. Consequently, some questions arise, Does God want it? Or does He permit it?

The answers to these questions are crucial. They disclose the nature of one's motives, the quality of one's claim to faith, either for a best or second-best faith, or mere human presumption apart from any divine revelation. Especially is this so in the light of George Vandeman's five reasons.

Read the following paragraphs from *Testimonies To Ministers,* and choose between what God really wants and what He seems only to permit. Choose between a first-best, mature faith in contrast to a second-best, immature, accommodating faith.

"Some have had a burden in regard to the wearing of a marriage ring, feeling that the wives of our ministers should conform to this custom. **All this is unnecessary.** Let the ministers' wives have the golden link which binds their souls to Jesus Christ, a pure and holy character, the true love and meekness and godliness that are fruit borne upon the Christian tree, and their influence will be secure anywhere. The fact that a disregard of the custom occasions remark is no good reason for adopting it.

"**We need not wear the sign,** for we are not untrue to our marriage vow, and the wearing of the ring would be no evidence that we were true. **I feel deeply over this leavening process which seems to be going on among us, in the conformity to custom and fashion. Not one penny should be spent for a circlet of gold to testify that we are married. In countries where the custom is imperative, we have no burden to condemn those who have their marriage ring; let them wear it if they can do so conscientiously.**"—*Testimonies to Ministers,* pp. 180, 181, emphasis supplied.

God, the Great Jeweler, wants *us* to be jewels. We should settle for nothing less than God's best. And how is this to be achieved? George Vandeman's five reasons are helpful. For they point to God as One who believes in jewelry. The best kind! In the right place! At the right time!

And remember, "All His biddings are enablings."[36] Says Jesus, "My grace is sufficient for thee."[37]

References

1. Revelation 3:18 with Revelation 19:8
2. Psalm 89:2 with Esther 8:5 and Numbers 15:38-39
3. Ezekiel 28:15-16 with 2 Peter 2:4 and Isaiah 14:12-14
4. Ezekiel 28:17-19 with Isaiah 14:12-14 and Jude 6
5. 1 Peter 2:21
6. Galatians 2:20
7. Romans 12:2
8. 1 John 2:6
9. Luke 6:46
10. 1 Corinthians 8:13, NIV
11. See Exodus 32:32
12. See Matthew 40, 41
13. John 16:13
14. See Matthew 16:24
15. See Genesis 34:30
16. See Exodus 32
17. Exodus 33:5, 6
18. Isaiah 51:16
19. Jeremiah 6:2
20. Isaiah 4:4
21. Jeremiah 6:2
22. 1 Timothy 2:9
23. 1 Peter 3:4
24. See Proverbs 30:12
25. Isaiah 3:16
26. See Isaiah 31:20, 21
27. See 2 Corinthians 6:17 and Revelation 18:4
28. See Romans 3:23
29. Daniel 12:1

30. See 2 Thessalonians 2:2-8
31. Isaiah 25:9
32. 1 Corinthians 13:12
33. See Malachi 3:17, 18
34. Isaiah 13:12
35. Matthew 19:8
36. E. G. White, *Christ's Object Lessons*, p. 333
37. 2 Corinthians 12:9